FINDING

A Visualized Study of Philemon

Dr. Allen D. Ferry

PREFACE

In 1984, for one of my last assignments at Dallas Theological Seminary, I read every commentary in the DTS library on *Philemon*.

Most commentaries about *Philemon* are bound in one volume with *Colossians*. Paul likely composed *Philemon* at roughly the same time that he wrote *Colossians* and *Ephesians*. The fact that both letters were carried by Onesimus and Tychicus to Philemon; the church likely assembled in Philemon's home, thus the commonality.

The variety of lessons taught in Philemon are basic but profound and life changing for individuals and the body of Christ, the church. Finding fellowship is a lofty goal in church associations. I have preached the concepts of this book in sermons in multiple settings: churches, camps, and prison. Every time, folks have expressed that biblical fellowship is missing today in churches; the most common response has been that previous to this study, the concept of fellowship only involved food!

The message of Philemon is that true fellowship requires two factors: a new birth and the new believer's acceptance by the body of believers. From the original study in 1984, my appreciation for this small book has grown significantly.

Several years ago, after speaking in chapel at Davis Bible College, a man approached me and with a smile quietly said, "**89-A-1894**" (not actual number). I immediately recognized the New York State format of the department identification number for inmates. (I was a chaplain for the Department of Corrections and Community Services for 13 years.)

89-A-1894

Inmate DIN
(Department Identification Number)
1989 = year person entered system
A = reception center
1894 = person of the year

We embraced as he told me he was a student at the college. His new life had eclipsed his former! Welcome to the family!

Finding Fellowship in prison seems difficult to imagine, seems far from possible but remember that several significant Bible characters were incarcerated.

For more extensive look at prison ministry, consider my book: *Insights from Inside*.

FOREWORD

In his excellent little book *Finding Fellowship – A Visualized Study of Philemon,* Dr. Allen Ferry has helped all of us to find fellowship!

Drawing from his rich background as Chaplain in prison ministry and in the military, Dr. Ferry has pictured real fellowship in difficult circumstances. He has done a careful study of the Book of Philemon and presents it well both academically and spiritually.

Many excellent charts and study questions are included and make the work valuable for the classroom, or the campfire. I heartily endorse it, and thank Dr. Ferry for the privilege.

Rev. Dr. John Y. Clagett
Th.M, D.Min.

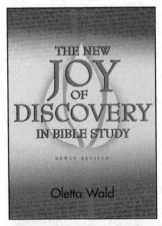

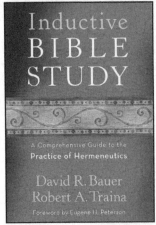

BOOKS WHICH FORMED THE AUTHOR'S METHOD OF INTERPRETATION.

The Joy of Discovery in Bible Study, 1975

Oletta Wald's basic principles of bible study are a must for students of the Word.

This approach is reading word by word while carefully looking at the text.

Inductive Bible Study, 1968

Robert Traina emphasizes letting the text speak for itself. He discourages reading into the text (eis·e·ge·ses), an interpretation that expresses the interpreter's own ideas, bias, or the like, rather than the meaning of the text.

Rather, Traina teaches that exegesis is the legitimate interpretation which "reads out of" the text what the original author or authors meant to convey."

Validity in Interpretation, 1967

E.D. Hirsch provides the logical premise for determining the actual textual meaning; the only valid interpretation is the author's intent.

Living by the Book, 1993

William D. & Howard G. Hendricks teach principles that make personal Bible study more fruitful and productive. You'll be challenged to read closely, probe more deeply, and learn how to make key observations that will bring fresh application to your life.

DEDICATION

Most parents desire for their children to do better than they have done. Theresa and I are no exception.

MARK is pastor of West Genesee Hills Baptist Church in Camillus, NY (2001-present). His preaching and teaching seriously exceeds my abilities. His use of visual presentations are awesome and demonstrate his understanding of the passages he teaches. Heather, Mark's wife, is an amazing partner and encourager. We are thankful for her ministry beside Mark.

JULAINE continues as an interpreter for the deaf (1997-present). Her abilities far exceed my sign language skills... hands down! She works from home, has an adopted son, Enoch, a high school senior, and serves in various church capacities.

Mark, Heather, and Julaine bring great joy to Theresa and me.

INTRODUCTION

This study will follow the Power Point slides I have developed to explain visually the thoughts of the Apostle Paul in his letter to Philemon.

To study any book of the Bible, read, read, read and notice the details. Although Philemon is a very short letter; while reading, first look for key words, powerful concepts, perhaps even unique features, then look for the big picture, main theme or subject.

In the 25 verses in Philemon, key words become obvious by repetition: beloved, love, heart total nine references to love! Lots of love here!

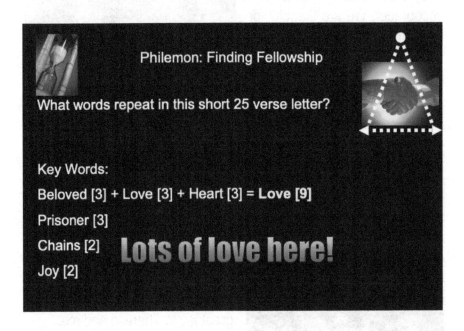

CONTENT

SECTION 1

Greeting

1 Paul, a prisoner of Christ Jesus, and Timothy our brother,

To Philemon our beloved friend and fellow laborer, 2 to the beloved Apphia, Archippus our fellow soldier, and to the church in your house:

3 Grace to you and peace from God our Father and the Lord Jesus Christ.

Paul was a prisoner in Rome, however, he viewed himself as that of a **prisoner/servant** of Christ. This is the only epistle in which he calls himself a prisoner; in seven of his letters he calls himself "an apostle." Here, he refrained from using the apostle title because this letter is a request not a command.

Prisoners usually see themselves negatively lacking freedom of choice, mobility, and normal family life. Paul viewed his life as fulfilling God's will, moving as the Lord directed, and living the life as a servant in the family of God.

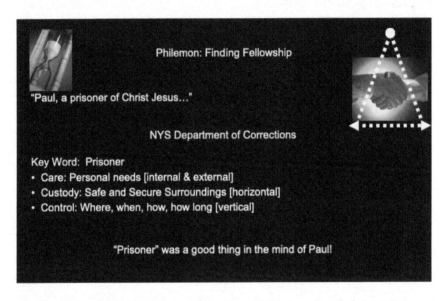

Philemon: Finding Fellowship

"Paul, a prisoner of Christ Jesus..."

NYS Department of Corrections

Key Word: Prisoner
- Care: Personal needs [internal & external]
- Custody: Safe and Secure Surroundings [horizontal]
- Control: Where, when, how, how long [vertical]

"Prisoner" was a good thing in the mind of Paul!

From my 13 years working for the NYS Department of Corrections, I learned the state (in theory) has three imperative words regarding prisoners: Care, Custody and Control. I find Paul's view the same of his incarceration!

Paul knew the Lord would care for his personal needs, keep him in safe and secure surroundings, and monitor his time in prison. And Epaphras was his fellow prisoner (v.23)

Paul had his experiences in prison and recognized the opportunity for witness and influence. He records this in the book of Philippians.

*But I want you to know, brethren, that the things which happened to me have actually turned out for the **furtherance of the gospel**, so that it has become evident to the whole palace guard, and to all the rest, that **my chains are in Christ**. —Phil. 1:12-13*

The love and grace of God changed Paul's life view. His adoption into the family of God gave him a spiritual father and brothers like Titus, Timothy, Philemon, etc.

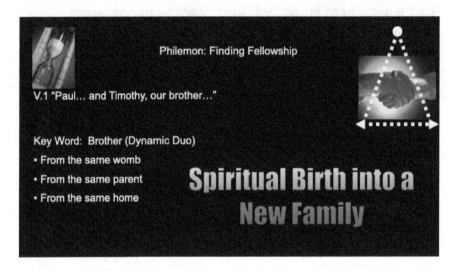

Philemon: Finding Fellowship

V.1 "Paul... and Timothy, our brother..."

Key Word: Brother (Dynamic Duo)
• From the same womb
• From the same parent
• From the same home

Spiritual Birth into a New Family

What exactly is a brother?

Brother comes from the Greek word, ἀδελφός (adelphos); ἀδελφός; from (as a connective particle) and δελφύς delphýs (the womb)i.e., a brother, whether born of the same two parents or only of the same father or mother; a brother (literally or figuratively) near or remote. [Thayer's Greek Lexicon][1]

Therefore, with the latitude of the word "womb", meanings include a person from the same womb, with the same parent, and/or from the same home.

Paul easily begins the letter to Philemon on the basis of love and brotherhood. More to come on this in later verses!

Philemon: Finding Fellowship

V.1-2 "Paul, a prisoner of Christ Jesus, and Timothy, our brother, to Philemon our beloved friend and fellow laborer, to the beloved Apphia, Archippus our fellow soldier, and to the church in your house..."

Key Words:
- Beloved [2] = the glue of the family
- Laborer = the goal of the family
- Soldier [endurance] = the grit of the family
- Church = the gathering of the family

Parallel & Eternal Reality

Sometimes, the actual words develop into a sermon outline, with obvious implications and application. Although these thoughts may not have been in Paul's mind or heart, these themes are universal in application.

Philemon: Finding Fellowship

V3 Grace to you and peace from God our Father and the Lord Jesus Christ.

Key Words:
- Grace: unmerited favor; KINDNESS without expected return
- Peace: condition of enjoyable existence w/o CONFLICT

It takes GRACE in church to have PEACE in church

Grace and peace are the Apostle Paul's normal greetings in his several letters.

Colossians, Ephesians, and Philippians begin with "Grace to you and peace from God our Father and the Lord Jesus Christ."

Peace is almost impossible without an abundance of grace. Paul clearly anticipated that Philemon needed grace regarding what his appeal would require.

Note Warren Wiersbe's outline of Philemon[2]:

I.   Appreciation (1-7) "I thank my God"

II. Appeal (8-16) **"I beseech thee"**

III. Assurance (17-25) "I will repay"

---

[1] Thayer, Joseph Henry, Thayer's Greek Lexicon. 1996

[2.] Wiersbe, Warren W., The Bible Exposition Commentary. Victor Books. 1989

SECTION 2

Philemon's Love and Faith

4 I thank my God, making mention of you always in my prayers, 5 hearing of your love and faith which you have toward the Lord Jesus and toward all the saints, 6 that the sharing of your faith may become effective by the acknowledgment of every good thing which is in you in Christ Jesus. 7 For we have great joy and consolation in your love, because the hearts of the saints have been refreshed by you, brother.

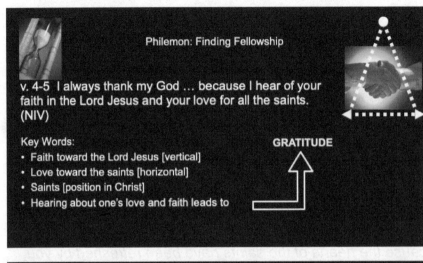

Philemon: Finding Fellowship

v. 4-5 I always thank my God ... because I hear of your faith in the Lord Jesus and your love for all the saints. (NIV)

Key Words:
- Faith toward the Lord Jesus [vertical]
- Love toward the saints [horizontal]
- Saints [position in Christ]
- Hearing about one's love and faith leads to

GRATITUDE

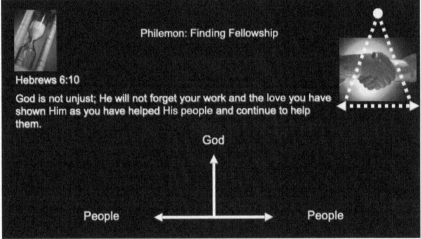

Philemon: Finding Fellowship

Hebrews 6:10

God is not unjust; He will not forget your work and the love you have shown Him as you have helped His people and continue to help them.

God

People   People

The author of Hebrews (perhaps the Apostle Paul) teaches that our **horizontal** relationships clearly demonstrate love for and gratitude to the Lord. Actually, this is underscored in numerous passages:

*Phil. 1:3—I **thank** my God upon every remembrance of **you**.*

*Colossians 1:9—For this reason we also, since the day we heard it, do not cease to **pray** for **you**, and to ask that you may be filled with the knowledge of **His will** in all wisdom and spiritual understanding…*

*Ephesians 1:15-16—Therefore I also, after I heard of your **faith in the Lord Jesus** and your love for all the saints, do not cease to give **thanks** for you, making mention of **you** in my prayers…*

*1 Thessalonians 1:2—We give **thanks** to God always for you all, making mention of **you** in our prayers…*

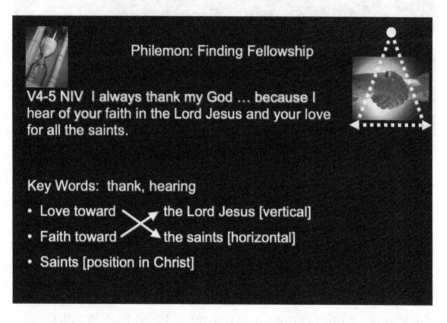

The NIV wording best visualizes the phenomenal truths in these two verses. Gratitude rises to God from what Paul has heard about Philemon.

Greek language experts call this verse construction a **chiasm** from Greek **chiasma**, a cross, named after the shape of the upper-case letter chi (**X**).

The construction places the **love** toward the saints as being initiated by **faith** toward the Lord Jesus. Love for the saints is horizontal but faith is vertical. Although, love could be for both, faith here is certainly in/toward the Lord.

This vertical/horizontal focus is often used by the Apostle Paul to emphasize the watchful and appreciative eye of the Lord regarding His own.

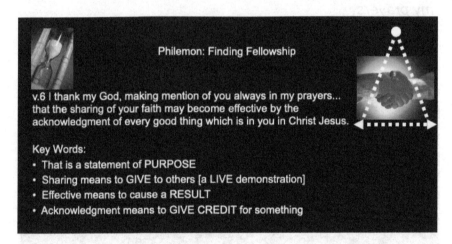

Philemon: Finding Fellowship

v.6 I thank my God, making mention of you always in my prayers... that the sharing of your faith may become effective by the acknowledgment of every good thing which is in you in Christ Jesus.

Key Words:
- That is a statement of PURPOSE
- Sharing means to GIVE to others [a LIVE demonstration]
- Effective means to cause a RESULT
- Acknowledgment means to GIVE CREDIT for something

Live demonstrations are the most effective witness of a changed life. These succinct four lines tell a sad truth.

To live above with saints we love;
oh that will be glory.
But to live below with saints we know;
well that's a different story. [Anonymous]

Sharing our faith requires every good thing to originate from Christ in us.

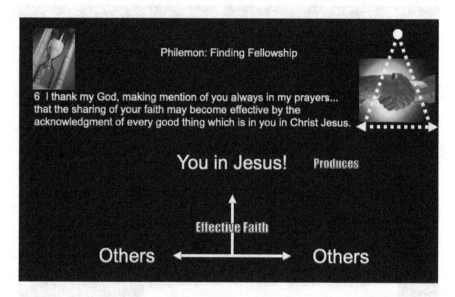

Philemon: Finding Fellowship

6 I thank my God, making mention of you always in my prayers... that the sharing of your faith may become effective by the acknowledgment of every good thing which is in you in Christ Jesus.

You in Jesus! Produces

Effective Faith

Others ⟷ Others

Paul is saying that when good things appear in us from Jesus, when this is acknowledged… this produces effective faith in others.

Our testimonies matter because we are observed by those around us. William J. Toms has said, "Be careful how you live. You may be the only Bible some person ever reads."

This was exactly what Paul was encouraging Philemon to do so that his faith might become effective.

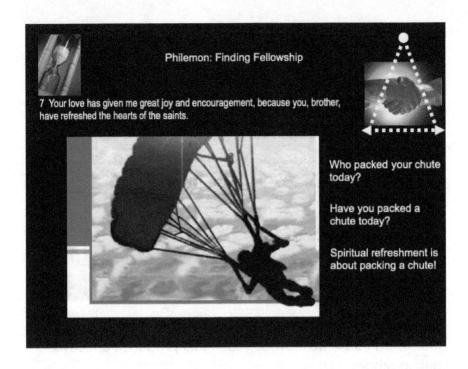

7 Your love has given me great joy and encouragement, because you, brother, have refreshed the hearts of the saints.

Who packed your chute today?

Have you packed a chute today?

Spiritual refreshment is about packing a chute!

Charles Plumb was a US Navy jet pilot in Vietnam. After 75 combat missions, his plane was destroyed by a surface-to-air missile. Plumb ejected and parachuted into enemy hands. He was captured and spent six years in a communist Vietnamese prison. He survived the ordeal and now lectures on lessons learned from that experience.

One day, when Plumb and his wife were sitting in a restaurant, a man at another table came up and said, "You're Plumb! You flew jet fighters in Vietnam from the aircraft carrier Kitty Hawk. You were shot down!"

"How in the world did you know that?" asked Plumb.

"I packed your parachute," the man replied.

Plumb gasped in surprise and gratitude. The man pumped his hand and said, "I guess it worked!" Plumb assured him,

"It sure did. If your chute hadn't worked, I wouldn't be here today."

Plumb couldn't sleep that night, thinking about that man. Plumb says, "I kept wondering what he might have looked like in a Navy uniform: a white hat, a bib in the back and bell-bottom trousers. I wonder how many times I might have seen him and not even said 'Good morning, how are you?' or anything, because, you see, I was a fighter pilot, and he was just a sailor."

Plumb thought of the man-hours the sailor had spent on a long wooden table in the bowels of the ship, carefully weaving the shrouds and folding the silks of each chute, holding in his hands each time the fate of someone he didn't know.

Who's Packing Your Parachute?

Now, Plumb asks his audience, "Who's packing your parachute?"

Everyone has someone who provides what they need to make it through the day. Plumb also points out that he needed many kinds of parachutes when his plane was shot down over enemy territory. He needed his physical parachute, his mental parachute, his emotional parachute and his spiritual parachute. He called on all these supports before reaching safety.

Sometimes in the daily challenges that life gives us, we miss what is really important.

We may fail to say "hello," "please," or "thank you," congratulate someone on something wonderful that has happened to them, give a compliment or just do something nice for no reason. (https://www.indres.com/news/who-packs-your-parachute-a-true-story-about-charles-plumb)[3]

7 Your love has given me great joy and encouragement, because you, brother, have refreshed the hearts of the saints.

Remember:

HAPPINESS is based on what happens

JOY is based on our relationships

Happiness is based on what happens; Joy is based on our relationships!

This simple but profound truth helps us to understand the loss of emotional stability in our society today. Happiness is lost so easily because of shifting norms of morality, reward, and circumstances.

In most grocery stores the refreshment shelves are perhaps the largest section: carbonated drinks 18%, coffee 10.8%, bottle water 25% hold the top three sellers. I have consumed my share of Pepsi but my long time favorite has been Dr. Pepper! Actually Dr. Pepper (1885) is older than Pepsi (1893) or Coke (1886). Of course, water is the best liquid refreshment because God created it in abundance!

However, historically the most satisfying refreshment is noted here by the Apostle Paul.

We need to praise what we want to flourish. Refreshment of the heart is a critical factor in joy. If we want to diminish the casualties of broken hearts, we need to praise people more!

Frankly, I believe that as believers our relationships in Christ are the main source of our joy in Him.

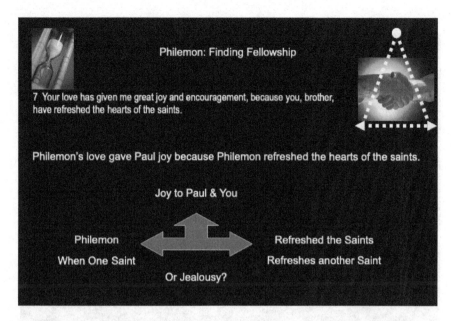

Philemon: Finding Fellowship

7 Your love has given me great joy and encouragement, because you, brother, have refreshed the hearts of the saints.

Philemon's love gave Paul joy because Philemon refreshed the hearts of the saints.

Joy to Paul & You

Philemon

When One Saint

Or Jealousy?

Refreshed the Saints

Refreshes another Saint

No man is an island, no man lives alone. These words by John Donne (1572-1631) capture the significant inter-connectivity between people. Hurting people often hurt others; Joyful people regularly encourage others directly or indirectly!

The Apostle Paul viewed the way Philemon's love for the saints within the church motivated joy in his heart as well as the hearts of the saints in his house/church. In Paul's own words, love gave joy to him and "spiritual" refreshment to the family members: brother to brother, sister to sister, sister to brother, and brother to sister.

This motivation of love cannot be over-emphasized that if we, as individuals, and collectively, as a church, want spiritual refreshment to flow from our relationships.

Of course, Paul is utilizing this wonderful situation as a positive prerequisite for the request that he is about to ask of Philemon.

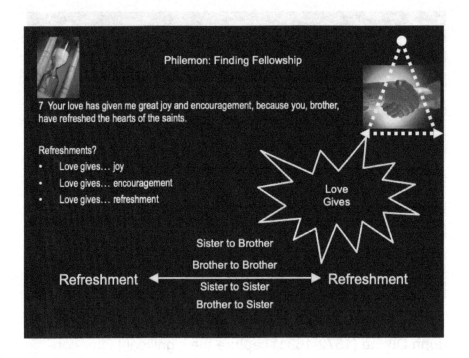

_____

[1] Toms, Williams. https://www.goodreads.com/quotes/439742-be-careful-how-you-live-you-may-be-the-only

[2] Wiersbe, Warren W., The Bible Exposition Commentary. Victor Books. 1989

[3] https://www.indres.com/news/who-packs-your-parachute-a-true-story-about-charles-plumb

SECTION 3

The Plea for Onesimus

8 Therefore, though I might be very bold in Christ to command you what is fitting, 9 yet for love's sake I rather appeal to you—being such a one as Paul, the aged, and now also a prisoner of Jesus Christ— 10 I appeal to you for my son Onesimus, whom I have begotten while in my chains, 11 who once was unprofitable to you, but now is profitable to you and to me.

12 I am sending him back. You therefore receive him, that is, my own heart, 13 whom I wished to keep with me, that on your behalf he might minister to me in my chains for the gospel. 14 But without your consent I wanted to do nothing, that your good deed might not be by compulsion, as it were, but voluntary.

15 For perhaps he departed for a while for this purpose, that you might receive him forever, 16 no longer as a slave but more than a slave—a beloved brother, especially to me but how much more to you, both in the flesh and in the Lord.

This section (verses 8-15) begins with the word "therefore" which begs the interpretive question: What is "therefore"... there for?" Therefore is a conjunctive adverb that means for that reason or cause, thus, or consequently.

Therefore is a hinge in thought that Paul uses to break between logical facts and for that reason, his conclusions.

Clearly, Paul could have boldly demanded for Philemon to do what he expected but instead he appealed on the basis of love. How come? Paul begins this section with "therefore" which logically refers to Philemon's testimony of providing love and spiritual refreshment to the brethren.

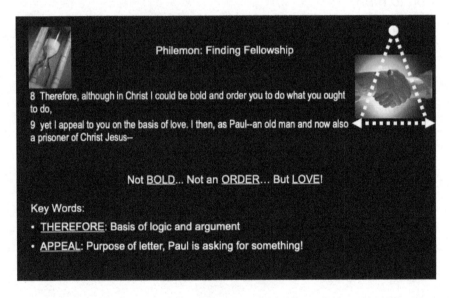

Philemon: Finding Fellowship

8 Therefore, although in Christ I could be bold and order you to do what you ought to do,

9 yet I appeal to you on the basis of love. I then, as Paul--an old man and now also a prisoner of Christ Jesus--

Not BOLD... Not an ORDER... But LOVE!

Key Words:
- THEREFORE: Basis of logic and argument
- APPEAL: Purpose of letter, Paul is asking for something!

Remember, Paul did not address this letter as an apostle in position but as a servant and brother. However, now he is going to make a request, an appeal.

When Paul makes his appeal, he mentions his age and that he is a prisoner. Is he asking for sympathy or empathy?

Philemon: Finding Fellowship

8 Therefore, although in Christ I could be bold and order you to do what you ought to do,

9 yet I appeal to you on the basis of love. I then, as Paul--an old man and now also a prisoner of Christ Jesus--

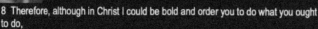

ELDER in Position and EXPERIENCE in Prison

Key Words:
- THEREFORE: Basis of logic and argument
- APPEAL: Purpose of letter, Paul is asking for something!
- SYMPATHY or EMPATHY?: Age, prisoner of Christ Jesus...

SYMPATHY:
1. the ability to enter into, understand, or share somebody else's feelings
2. the feelings of somebody who enters into or shares another's feelings
3. the feeling or expression of pity or sorrow for the pain or distress of somebody else
4. the inclination to think or feel the same as somebody else
5. agreement or harmony with something or somebody else

It seems important to Paul to ask Philemon for consideration considering his age and incarceration. Not sympathy but **empathy** with his feelings and difficulties.

EMPATHY:
1. the ability to identify with and understand another person's feelings or difficulties
2. the transfer of your own feelings and emotions to an object such as a painting

A lesson learned here is that we need to have empathy for the situations of others. Paul was a leader and wanted others to follow him with understanding that he was getting older and was incarcerated. He was not seeking sympathy!

These are good questions raised for understanding Paul's appeal and potentially ours in future situations. Paul wanted Philemon to understand his feelings for Onesimus and his motivation for the pending request.

Like Paul, our lives are to influence, encourage, and inspire others toward better behavior and choices in Christian living.

I want EMPATHY not sympathy!

1. Do people identify with what I feel?
2. Do people understand my motivation?
3. Does my maturity influence people toward better behavior?
4. Does my life experience encourage and inspire people?

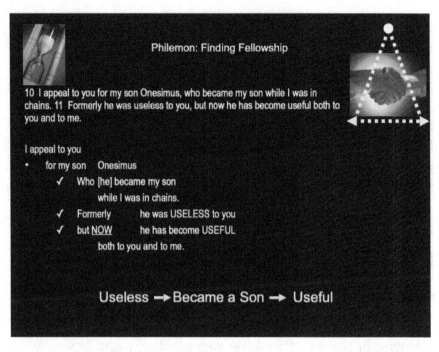

Philemon: Finding Fellowship

10 I appeal to you for my son Onesimus, who became my son while I was in chains. 11 Formerly he was useless to you, but now he has become useful both to you and to me.

I appeal to you
- for my son   Onesimus
    - ✓ Who [he] became my son
          while I was in chains.
    - ✓ Formerly   he was USELESS to you
    - ✓ but NOW   he has become USEFUL
          both to you and to me.

Useless → Became a Son → Useful

Paul is appealing to Philemon for Onesimus in two ways. What has happened?

First, Onesimus spiritually became Paul's son while he was incarcerated. Sonship speaks of birth into Paul's family! The name Onesimus comes from the Greek adjective Ὀνήσιμος (Onēsimos), meaning "useful, profitable, beneficial." Onesimus is now useful to both Paul and Philemon.

Second, the Apostle Paul became a spiritual father to Onesimus who most likely was also incarcerated. Paul's family was growing.

Useless people can became both sons, daughters and useful. Potential lies in each and all to become believers in Christ and mutually beneficial to the church family.

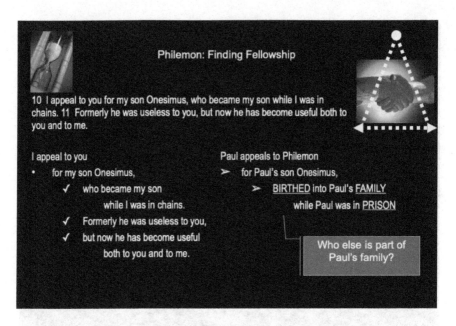

Philemon: Finding Fellowship

10 I appeal to you for my son Onesimus, who became my son while I was in chains. 11 Formerly he was useless to you, but now he has become useful both to you and to me.

I appeal to you
- for my son Onesimus,
  - ✓ who became my son
    while I was in chains.
  - ✓ Formerly he was useless to you,
  - ✓ but now he has become useful
    both to you and to me.

Paul appeals to Philemon
- ➤ for Paul's son Onesimus,
  - ➤ BIRTHED into Paul's FAMILY
    while Paul was in PRISON

Who else is part of Paul's family?

This raises the question: "Who else is part of Paul's family?" Remember that in verse 1, he was spiritually and biblically correct to call Timothy "our" brother implying that Philemon was also a brother.

The Apostle is moving toward the purpose of this letter; he is establishing the "family" relationship that salvation and each new birth creates. Jesus taught that new birth, being born again is essential. (See Final Thought, page 65)

Jesus answered and said to him, "Most assuredly, I say to you, unless one is born again, he cannot see the kingdom of God." —John 3:3

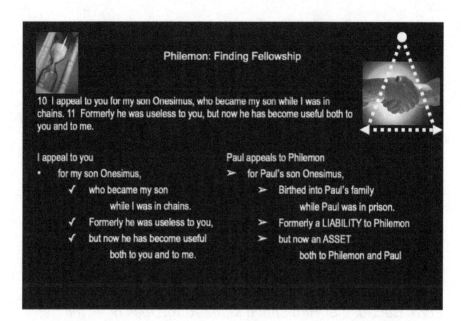

Philemon: Finding Fellowship

10 I appeal to you for my son Onesimus, who became my son while I was in chains. 11 Formerly he was useless to you, but now he has become useful both to you and to me.

I appeal to you
- for my son Onesimus,
  - ✓ who became my son
    while I was in chains.
  - ✓ Formerly he was useless to you,
  - ✓ but now he has become useful
    both to you and to me.

Paul appeals to Philemon
- ➤ for Paul's son Onesimus,
  - ➤ Birthed into Paul's family
    while Paul was in prison.
  - ➤ Formerly a LIABILITY to Philemon
  - ➤ but now an ASSET
    both to Philemon and Paul

Paul challenged Philemon to remember this relationship with him and now his son, Onesimus. Because, spiritually speaking, Onesimus now is Philemon's nephew and both are members of the same family!

It has been said that God has no grandchildren only children by birth. However, by evangelism, spiritual reproduction takes place. When we lead someone to Christ for salvation as Paul did with Onesimus—the family enlarges and God has more children!

Following this logically, in a spiritual relationship, if Paul and Philemon are brothers, then Onesimus has become Philemon's nephew! A new family member gives Philemon a new responsibility for his nephew!

Paul also wants Philemon to recognize the great change in his financial assets by Onesimus' change of status!

The Apostle Paul acknowledges that formerly Onesimus was useless and a serious liability to Philemon. His insight is also based in his own experience. He writes to the saints in Philippi:

Philippians 3:8

*But more than that, I count everything as **loss** compared to the priceless privilege and supreme advantage of knowing Christ Jesus my Lord [and of growing more deeply and thoroughly acquainted with Him—a joy unequaled]. For His sake I have lost everything, and I consider it all **garbage**, so that I may gain Christ… AMP*

*More than that, I also consider everything to be a **loss** in view of the surpassing value of knowing Christ Jesus my Lord. Because of Him I have suffered the loss of all things and consider them **filth**, so that I may gain Christ… HCSB*

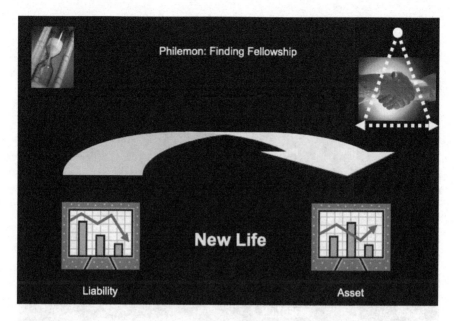

Philemon: Finding Fellowship

New Life

Liability

Asset

The Apostle Paul reminds Philemon that formerly Onesimus was useless and a serious liability. The contrast is between before and after salvation. Onesimus is now an asset in his new life.

*For the wages of sin is **death**, but the gift of God is eternal life in Christ Jesus our Lord. —Rom. 6:23*

*Moreover the law entered that the offense might abound. But where sin abounded, grace abounded much more, so that as sin reigned in **death**, even so grace might reign through righteousness to **eternal life** through Jesus Christ our Lord. —Rom. 5:20-21*

The value of human life is held in stark contrast in these verses, from life to death is certainly a statement of value.

In the following verses I want you to see the implications of the letter for the church as a family. Although Paul only specifically writes to Philemon, please understand the lessons of importance we need to learn.

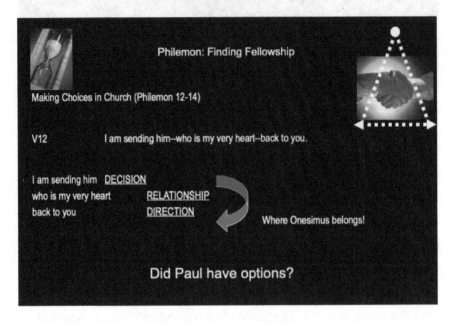

Philemon: Finding Fellowship

Making Choices in Church (Philemon 12-14)

V12   I am sending him—who is my very heart—back to you.

I am sending him DECISION
who is my very heart   RELATIONSHIP
back to you   DIRECTION

Where Onesimus belongs!

Did Paul have options?

Paul had two options:
Option 1—Selfish
Option 2—Unselfish
He considered both and decided on option #2

When the Apostle Paul decides to return Onesimus to Philemon, he does this within the context of the local church assembly. I believe the church was meeting in Philemon's home. His actions would be observed by those attending. He had to consider watchful eyes always focus on leadership. How he treated this slave, whether harshly or graciously would be significant.

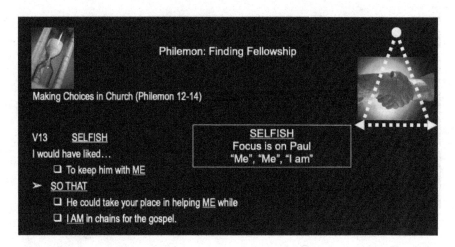

Philemon: Finding Fellowship

Making Choices in Church (Philemon 12-14)

V13   SELFISH
I would have liked...
  ❑ To keep him with ME
➤ SO THAT
  ❑ He could take your place in helping ME while
  ❑ I AM in chains for the gospel.

SELFISH
Focus is on Paul
"Me", "Me", "I am"

His first choice would have been selfish with the benefits for himself. The lesson learned here is the best decisions are not selfish. The second choice was unselfish. Paul teaches by example the biblical principle "others first." Paul could have been selfish but chose to be unselfish.

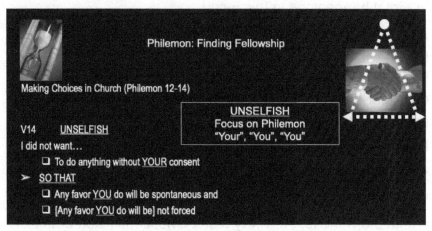

Philemon: Finding Fellowship

Making Choices in Church (Philemon 12-14)

UNSELFISH
Focus on Philemon
"Your", "You", "You"

V14   UNSELFISH
I did not want...
  ❑ To do anything without YOUR consent
➤ SO THAT
  ❑ Any favor YOU do will be spontaneous and
  ❑ [Any favor YOU do will be] not forced

He also wrote: ***Let nothing be done through selfish*** *ambition or conceit, but in lowliness of mind let each esteem **others** better than himself. Let each of you look out not only for his own interests, but also for the interests of **others**.— Phil. 2:3-4*

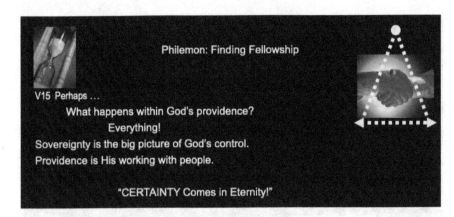

Philemon: Finding Fellowship

V15 Perhaps ...
What happens within God's providence?
Everything!
Sovereignty is the big picture of God's control.
Providence is His working with people.

"CERTAINTY Comes in Eternity!"

Verse 15 captures the tension within God's sovereignty when Pauls says, "Perhaps the reason."

Perhaps can mean about the same thing as maybe: things that perhaps could happen may happen, or they might not.

In the divine picture, in God's view, some things are meant to be, to happen within His **sovereignty**. He is in control of the total happenings in this world.

In the human perspective, He works **providentially** with people! We cannot be certain until we view life in the rearview mirror.

Consider this situation with Philemon and Onesimus, what happened could have been prevented. Perhaps, Perhaps...

Even hindsight is not always 20/20.

- Why did Onesimus have to meet Paul to be saved?

- Why didn't Philemon witness better in the first place?

- If he did witness, then why didn't Onesimus listen better?

- Why didn't Paul disciple Philemon better regarding evangelism?

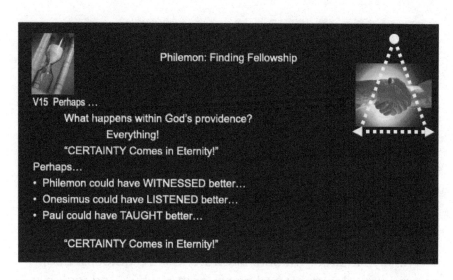

These are unanswerable questions much like we do today when we ask "WHY" so often! **Certainty comes in eternity** but the Lord does provide a rational answer for Philemon.

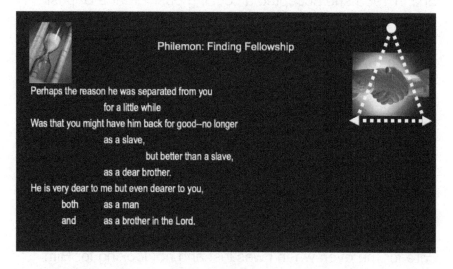

Why do bad things happen to good people or why do good things happen to bad people? When God is working, good things happen!

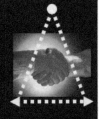

Perhaps the reason he was separated from you
for a little while
Was that you might have him back for good—

Why do bad things happen to good people?
When God is working... good things happen!
Perhaps the reason...   God is GOOD all the time...
        was to DEMONSTRATE that...   All the time, God is GOOD all the time...

We always look for rational answers to life's detours! Look at my spiritual journey and discover the "why" God took me on a three-year life detour.

It was 1962 when my parents divorced. Mom needed work and in 1963 she accepted a cooking position at a Baptist Camp on Lake Chautauqua, NY. I was thrilled about the water skiing and fishing opportunities but no spiritual thoughts in mind. She would not accept the position until the camp agreed to hired me!

Separation from my father was very painful but after I was saved, God provided a very special man named Reverend Ernest Hook to disciple me. Three years without Dad but three years with Pastor Hook were a significant tradeoff for my eternal benefit.

"Perhaps" never occurred to me at the time but looking back this verse speaks loudly about the Lord's providential care for me even when I was lost and not looking for Him.

(Theologically, this is called "prevenient grace" which is a theological concept that refers to the grace of God in a person's life which precedes and prepares to conversion.)

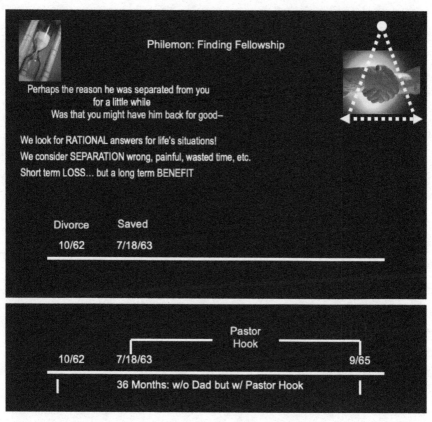

Philemon: Finding Fellowship

Perhaps the reason he was separated from you
for a little while
Was that you might have him back for good--

We look for RATIONAL answers for life's situations!
We consider SEPARATION wrong, painful, wasted time, etc.
Short term LOSS... but a long term BENEFIT

Divorce	Saved
10/62	7/18/63

Pastor
Hook

10/62	7/18/63		9/65

36 Months: w/o Dad but w/ Pastor Hook

I sincerely believe the Lord providentially cared for me and my future throughout the divorce, working at Bethany Camp and three year separation from Dad but three wonderful years learning from Reverend Ernest Hook, my first pastor.

Sin ruins lives; however God rescues and replaces with purposeful living.

SECTION 4

Philemon's Obedience Encouraged

17 If then you count me as a partner, receive him as you would me. 18 But if he has wronged you or owes anything, put that on my account. 19 I, Paul, am writing with my own hand. I will repay—not to mention to you that you owe me even your own self besides. 20 Yes, brother, let me have joy from you in the Lord; refresh my heart in the Lord.

21 Having confidence in your obedience, I write to you, knowing that you will do even more than I say. 22 But, meanwhile, also prepare a guest room for me, for I trust that through your prayers I shall be granted to you.

Partner is a huge word in this short letter with significant implications.

*So... if you consider me a **partner**, welcome Onesimus as you would me!* Why? Because Paul, Philemon and Onesimus are together in this family.

The word in the Greek is koinonia, and is translated into English as **communion**, **fellowship**, and **partner** as here.

Fellowship is shared participation within a community.

Will folks attending our church find fellowship? Of course, we say. But do we accept everyone? Or only those we see as acceptable?

Welcome is often qualified by personal opinions: unfair bias against dress, hairstyles, behavior, and even age! Everyone has a choice to make about new people in church even before Christian testimony is known or established.

Accept or Reject? Seems easy to answer until someone we perceive as not worthy, unsavory sits near us. Perhaps a guy with blue hair, nose ring, torn jeans, and multiple tattoos just can't be acceptable!

So, who is sitting next to you? How about this guy? A bit strange hair style! Would you move a little farther away?

Perhaps... but this photo is of my son in days long ago.

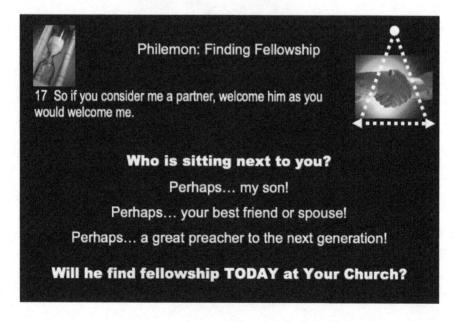

Philemon: Finding Fellowship

17 So if you consider me a partner, welcome him as you would welcome me.

Who is sitting next to you?

Perhaps... my son!

Perhaps... your best friend or spouse!

Perhaps... a great preacher to the next generation!

Will he find fellowship TODAY at Your Church?

Do we judge hair styles we dislike as disqualifying men and women from "our" fellowship?

These are worthy questions needed to understand this book of Philemon. How we accept new family members may be the encouragement or lack thereof that determines their future.

Finding Fellowship is the purpose of this letter; Paul wants Onesimus to find fellowship with Philemon. By simple implication and application, the Lord wants new believers to find fellowship in churches.

Will you do your part?

Perhaps this challenge to act properly will motivate, when you realize that the new person in church just may become your best friend or spouse in days ahead, a godly church leader or perhaps a a great preacher to the next generation.

But only will happen when we receive people like Paul was expecting Philemon to accept and receive Onesimus!

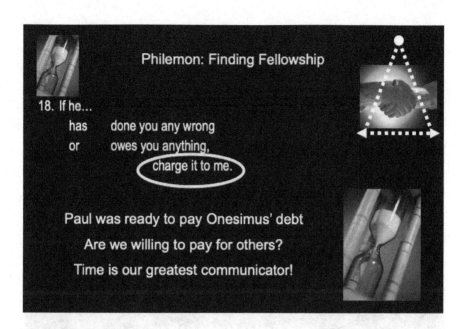

Philemon: Finding Fellowship

18. If he...
    has   done you any wrong
    or   owes you anything,
           charge it to me.

Paul was ready to pay Onesimus' debt

Are we willing to pay for others?

Time is our greatest communicator!

Theologians call this the doctrine of imputation: to impute means "to put it on account." (Paul fully explains this doctrine in Romans 5.)

Warren Wiersbe explains imputation:

> When Jesus Christ died on the cross, my sins were **put on His account**, and He was treated the way I should have been treated. When I trusted Him as my Savior, His righteousness was **put on my account**, and now God accepts me in Jesus Christ. Jesus said to the Father, "He no longer owes You a debt because I paid it fully on the cross. Receive him as You would receive Me. Let him come into the family circle!"[1]

Here in Philemon, however, he is making imputation personal by applying the concept between Philemon, Onesimus, and himself. Paul asks Philemon **if** Onesimus has done wrong or owes him anything, charge it to him.

Paul's willingness to be a living example of imputation is a great testimony to his understanding of this cardinal doctrine and practical application. Philemon would have certainly recognized the doctrinal terminology and heavy implication he was to accept and apply.

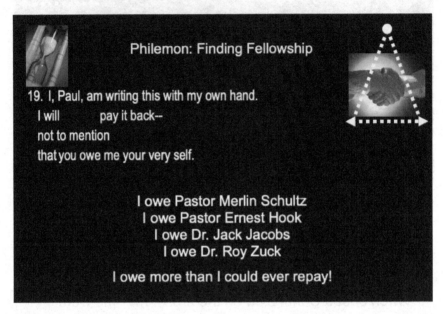

Philemon: Finding Fellowship

19. I, Paul, am writing this with my own hand.
I will   pay it back--
not to mention
that you owe me your very self.

I owe Pastor Merlin Schultz
I owe Pastor Ernest Hook
I owe Dr. Jack Jacobs
I owe Dr. Roy Zuck

I owe more than I could ever repay!

Pastor Schultz explained the gospel the night I was saved. Pastor Hook was my first pastor/mentor. Dr. Jacobs was my dearest bible professor. Dr. Zuck was my most impressive seminary professor.

I can pay forward what I owe to them. The next generation requires Christ-like mentors with time to invest because time is our greatest asset and communicator!

In a very real sense, I have been joyfully paying my debt to these men and others by decades of ministry stemming out of sincere appreciation for the time and love they shared with me!

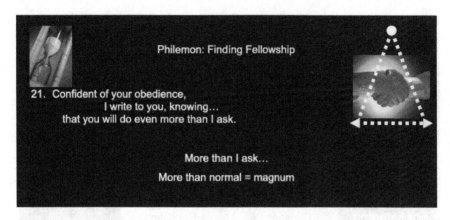

21. Confident of your obedience,
   I write to you, knowing...
   that you will do even more than I ask.

More than I ask...

More than normal = magnum

Paul chooses to use the Greek word "hyper" (translated more than) to emphasize his hope and expectation that Philemon would **do more than** what he is asking. Hyper is what we want to emulate in our lives for Christ.

When I realized that "hyper" and 'magnum" share the thought of being great, large, big... more so than normal, my thoughts instantly went to my revolver in .357 magnum. It is a magnum because it is more powerful than the original .38 Special. How much so is easily seen, only .135 inches.

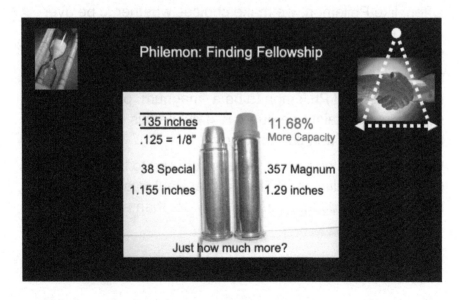

Philemon: Finding Fellowship

.135 inches
.125 = 1/8"

11.68%
More Capacity

38 Special
1.155 inches

.357 Magnum
1.29 inches

Just how much more?

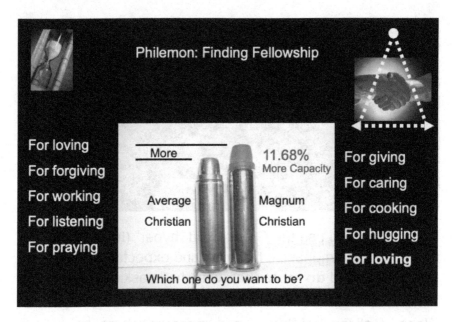

Philemon: Finding Fellowship

For loving
For forgiving
For working
For listening
For praying

More | 11.68% More Capacity

Average Christian | Magnum Christian

Which one do you want to be?

For giving
For caring
For cooking
For hugging
For loving

Study the difference and think about your life. Do you desire to be magnum or satisfied to be ordinary/average?

Seems like a small difference but the .357 Magnum has 11.68% more capacity for powder/accelerant and thus velocity and resulting energy downrange!

Often, like Philemon, we make choices whether to be average or exceptional, to be a magnum believer. The visual says to quite well. Do we have more capacity for loving, forgiving, listening, giving, caring, cooking, hugging, **loving**?

Paul challenged Philemon to be a "magnum" person toward Onesimus! Certainly we ought to emulate this in our lives both personally and corporately.

We have to ask ourselves, "Are we striving to be magnum toward other believers?" This is what Paul was asking of Philemon toward Onesimus, to do more than average.

Philemon: Finding Fellowship

22. And one thing more:
   Prepare a guest room for me,
      because I hope to be restored to you
         in answer to your prayers.

• Preparation   Why would Philemon prepare for Paul?

Is this a suggestion for Philemon to prepare a guest room for Onesimus?

Remember how Paul described himself as a partner? His challenge here is for Philemon to think about ways as a partner, he should prepare, pray and welcome him and by implication, also prepare for Onesimus!

Will he *Find Fellowship*? Would we accept Onesimus?

Philemon: Finding Fellowship

22. And one thing more:
   Prepare a guest room for me,
      because I hope to be restored to you
         in answer to your prayers.

• Preparation
• Anticipation
• Intercession   Why would Philemon pray for Paul?

Is this a suggestion for Philemon to pray for Onesimus as he would Paul?

Richardson now Paul's-Cross; and as a mark of p...
thanks to you such fortune served, that they saw in t...
nearer ... ehe latter open... spacious somewhere ling a...
multitude of it... Raleigh of Charles a...

ABOVE: 22 Fulton somewhere A. Edward cat a twenty-s...

SECTION 5

Farewell

23 Epaphras, my fellow prisoner in Christ Jesus, greets you,
24 as do Mark, Aristarchus, Demas, Luke, my fellow labor-
ers.

25 The grace of our Lord Jesus Christ be with your spirit.
Amen.

Philemon: Finding Fellowship

23. Epaphras,
      my fellow prisoner in Christ Jesus,
            sends you greetings.
24. And so do Mark, Aristarchus, Demas and Luke,
      my fellow workers.
25. The grace of the Lord Jesus Christ
            be with your spirit.

Final Challenge
- Surrender to the Lord
- Serve the Lord

2 Timothy 4:9

Be diligent to come to me quickly; for Demas has forsaken me, having loved this PRESENT world, and has departed...

Philemon: Finding Fellowship

23. Epaphras,
      my fellow prisoner in Christ Jesus,
            sends you greetings.
24. And so do Mark, Aristarchus, Demas and Luke,
      my fellow workers.
25. The grace of the Lord Jesus Christ
            be with your spirit.

Final Challenge
- Surrender to the Lord
- Serve the Lord
- Separate unto the Lord

1 John 2:15
Do not love the world or anything in the world. If anyone loves the world, the love of the Father is not in him.

Sadly, not all who begin the race finish it. Some start and fall prey to distractions of this world. The key word here is this **present** world. It does offer much now but lacks eternal perspective.

The final challenge here rises from the life of Demas, Paul's fellow worker, who later leaves him, having a greater love for his present world. Sadly, if a fellow worker of Paul was drawn into the love of the world… we best be diligent.

Separation is often the best option! Surrender to the Lord, serve the Lord, and then separate!

For all that is in the world—the lust of the flesh, the lust of the eyes, and the pride of life—is not of the Father but is of the world. —1 John 2:16

Therefore let him who thinks he stands take heed lest he fall. —1 Cor. 10:12

SECTION 6

Finding Fellowship
In Action

Philemon: Finding Fellowship

How did Onesimus find fellowship with Paul?

By BIRTH into a family he became his SON!

Paul & Onesimus

Philemon: Finding Fellowship

How did Onesimus find fellowship with Philemon?

By BIRTH into a family they became BROTHERS!

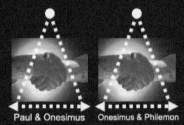

Paul & Onesimus   Onesimus & Philemon

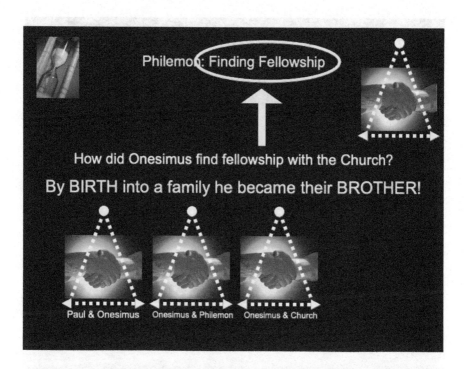

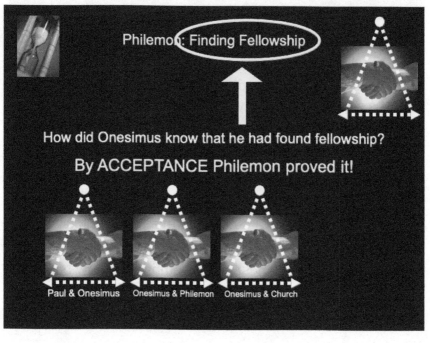

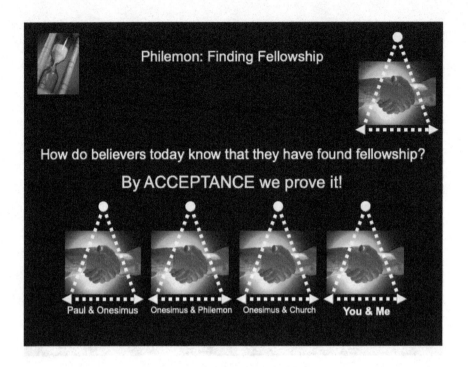

The visuals on each slide are important!

How do believers today know they have fellowship?

The Hourglass—time is our greatest means of investment. Personality, education, or position mean little without sharing our lives, our time with new believers.

The Handshake—the close extended hand demonstrates our friendship and fellowship with new believers.

The Triangle—the three-way relationship between the new believer, the Lord, and ourselves is true biblical fellowship.

Do new believers today know they have found fellowship?

This challenge raises these questions: are we investing our time, extending our friendship, and embracing new believers as in the lord.

SECTION 7

DISCUSSION QUESTIONS

DISCUSSION QUESTIONS

1 Paul, a prisoner of Christ Jesus, and Timothy, our brother, to Philemon our beloved friend and fellow laborer, 2 to the beloved Apphia, Archippus our fellow soldier, and to the church in your house…

Principles of Biblical Understanding

1. Why is observation the first step in understanding the Bible?

2. What did you notice as we read the text together? Compare observations and personal reflections.

3. What word or phase jumped out at you? Why? Explain.

4. What words are repeated in the 25 verses of Philemon?

   [Prisoner, Brother, Joy, Beloved, Heart]

5. What seems initially to be the big idea of the letter to Philemon?

DISCUSSION QUESTIONS

***

Understanding Philemon

1. What benefits/blessings do you have as a **prisoner** of Jesus Christ?

   [Care, Custody, Control]

2. Why do you think Paul began his letter with this concept? (Eph. 3:1; 4:1; 2 Tim. 1:8)

3. What does a good **brother** do for you?

4. Share how a **friend** pulled you through a difficult time?

5. Why is friendship important in the local church?

6. Why does **labor** (working together) pull people together in a local church?

7. Perhaps what significant aspect of **soldiering** does Paul suggest by using this word (2 Tim. 2:3)?

8. Perhaps why does Paul greet the **church** in Philemon's house?

9. Perhaps how does the church provide a form of account-ability?

10. What does having a church in their home say about Philemon and Apphia?

11. Is anything preventing your home from becoming a place of ministry?

DISCUSSION QUESTIONS

---

10 I appeal to you for my son Onesimus, who became my son while I was in chains. 11 Formerly he was useless to you, but now he has become useful both to you and to me.

Discovering the Meaning of Philemon

1. Was Onesimus actually Paul's biological **son**? If not, how are they related?

2. If you are born again, you are a child of God and in the family of God. What are benefits of this family relationship?

3. If you were Onesimus how would you feel about Paul?

4. Through spiritual birth **useless** Onesimus became a **useful** person. List what makes your life "in Christ" useful or profitable.

5. What makes someone a **liability** at home and at church? What can you do at home and church that would make you an **asset**?

6. **Chains** did not stop Paul's evangelism. What are the most common barriers for you to witness? How can you begin to break the chains that hold you back?

DISCUSSION QUESTIONS

---

12 I am sending him--who is my very heart--back to you. 13 I would have liked to keep him with me so that he could take your place in helping me while I am in chains for the gospel. 14 But I did not want to do anything without your consent, so that any favor you do will be spontaneous and not forced.

1. Think about your individual relationships; how many do you describe as "your very heart?" Why not more?

2. What have you done to serve those who have less freedom, i.e., the elderly, the handicapped, the incarcerated, the sick, etc.?

3. Have you ever thought of taking someone's place for a day or week to give him or her a rest or perhaps offer to care for children to give a couple a night out? Discuss

4. Ministry cannot be without manners! Think about how gratitude, appreciation, and kind requests would make life in church better.

5. Where do spontaneous actions fit into church life?

6. When do favors best benefit the church?

DISCUSSION QUESTIONS

---

15 Perhaps the reason he was separated from you for a little while was that you might have him back for good—16 no longer as a slave, but better than a slave, as a dear brother. He is very dear to me but even dearer to you, both as a man and as a brother in the Lord.

1. Why was Onesimus' situation bad? What did Joseph say later about how his brothers had treated him years earlier? (Gen. 45:7-8; 50:19-21) Describe a situation in your life that seemed "bad" that actually turned out for good.

2. What do we become after we exercise faith in Christ Jesus? (Gal. 3:26-28)

3. What is the basic requirement for church "family" membership? Is everyone welcome? (1 Cor. 12:12-14) Remember: Onesimus is returning to the church in Philemon's home. Discuss why you think he will or will not be welcome?

4. How can one be free while a slave or incarcerated? To what are believers called? (1 Cor. 7:20-24)

5. How is work an opportunity to please the Lord and our employer? (Eph. 6:5-9; Col. 4:1)

6. Would you now describe Paul's incarceration as good? Was it good that Paul met Onesimus while in prison? (Rom. 8:28)

7. Discus the implications of how Paul wants Philemon to view Onesimus?

DISCUSSION QUESTIONS

17 So if you consider me a partner, welcome him as you would welcome me.

1. Read 2 Corinthians 8:23-24. Why does Paul challenge the church to show love for one another in the Lord? Who gets the honor from this?

2. Read Philippians 2:19-22. List several ways Timothy demonstrated his genuine love for Paul and the church.

3. Read 1 Thessalonians 3: 6-10. List ways they encouraged one another? What "good news story" can you tell about our church? What pleasant memories do you have from church?

4. Read 1 Thessalonians 5:25-27. What are more ways you can encourage one another? Don't get too personal here!

5. Read James 2:1-4. How should we treat the strangers who attend your church? List ways you can make all visitors welcome.

6. Read John 13:34-35. How does a true disciple best demonstrate his relationship with Christ, in the family, in the community, and at work?

DISCUSSION QUESTIONS

17 So if you consider me a partner, welcome him as you would welcome me.

1. How would we accept the Apostle Paul today if he came to your church? What makes him special?

2. How does Paul challenge Philemon to welcome or accept Onesimus? (2 Cor. 8:23-24)

3. List several ways Philemon may have demonstrated love for Paul and the church (the family of God)? (Phil. 2:19-22)

4. In the history of most churches, children, teens, adults attend, come and go. Saved or unsaved, how would we receive them if they return? (James 2:1-4)

5. What is the proof, the evidence of a true disciple? What does he/she look like? (John 13:34-35)

DISCUSSION QUESTIONS

---

18 If he has done you any wrong or owes you anything, charge it to me. 19 I, Paul, am writing this with my own hand. I will pay it back--not to mention that you owe me your very self. 20 I do wish, brother, that I may have some benefit from you in the Lord; refresh my heart in Christ. 21 Confident of your obedience, I write to you, knowing that you will do even more than I ask.

1. It seems that Philemon owed a debt to Philemon. How does debt stress relationships?

2. Read Romans 13:7-8. List several ways that you can owe something to someone you have never met? How does debt motivate some people?

3. Read Romans 5:13, 17-18. How did mankind become sinful and how does mankind become righteous? What does "impute" mean? What key fact defines a gift?

4. Is this a personal message or just a form letter?

5. Read Philippians 4:1, 1 Thessalonians 2:20. List several ways someone has "blessed" you or spiritually "refreshed" or been a "joy" to you. What is the difference between "joy" and "happiness" in your thinking?

6. What helps grow your confidence in people? What makes some people do more than is asked of them?

Discussion Questions

---

18 If he has done you any wrong or owes you anything, charge it to me. 19 I, Paul, am writing this with my own hand. I will pay it back--not to mention that you owe me your very self. 20 I do wish, brother, that I may have some benefit from you in the Lord; refresh my heart in Christ. 21 Confident of your obedience, I write to you, knowing that you will do even more than I ask.

1. What are the names of those who have visited your class in the past few weeks? Who were they visiting? Where are their homes? What did you learn about them?

2. How can you do a better job of making visitors feel welcome?

3. It seems that Philemon owed a debt to Philemon. How does debt stress relationships? (V18)

4. How does a hand written note mean more that a form letter addressed "To Occupant"? Is this a personal message or just a form letter? (V19)

5. What helps grow your confidence in people? What makes some people do more than is asked of them? (V21)

DISCUSSION QUESTIONS

---

²² And one thing more: Prepare a guest room for me, because I hope to be restored to you in answer to your prayers. ²³ Epaphras, my fellow prisoner in Christ Jesus, sends you greetings. ²⁴ And so do Mark, Aristarchus, Demas and Luke, my fellow workers. ²⁵ The grace of the Lord Jesus Christ be with your spirit.

1. Does a pending visit of a friend to your home raise your anticipation and nervousness?
2. List why you can be hopeful in prayer? What are you praying for?
3. Why does friendship in Christ thrive in difficult circumstances?
4. How does working together create strong friendship?
5. Is it possible for friendships in Christ to fail? (2 Tim. 4:9-11) What do you think happened to Demas?
6. Why is grace necessary for spiritual success?

Perhaps...

You have now finished reading this book and are asking yourself, "Why is my current painful life situation happening?" What can I learn from my health issues, heartaches, disappointments, misery, and the list goes on and on?

A simple thought, "He [the Father] makes His sun rise on the evil and on the good, and sends rain on the just and on the unjust" (Mat. 5:45). We live in a world where natural disasters affect all.

God's Word provides two excellent examples of His providential supervision and care of our lives.

In the biblical book named after her, Esther is a young Jewish woman who finds favor with the king, becomes queen, and risks her life to save the Jewish people from destruction. Esther went before the king prepared for the worst case scenario but she got even more than expected! Many people became followers of God! Esther was in a very difficult, a life threatening situation. The Lord had placed her exactly in the right place at the right time.

The text tells us, "Yet who knows whether you have come to the kingdom for such a time as this?" (Esther 4:14). The Lord knew. Esther's obedience was key to the salvation of the Jews!

More familiar may be the story of Joseph: hated by his brothers, sold into slavery, and long-time separation from family. However, his faithfulness to the Lord, and willingness to forgive and see the bigger picture, he said, "But as for you [his brothers], you meant evil against me; but God meant it for good, in order to bring it about as it is this day, to save many people alive" (Gen. 50:20).

You may not see a future blessing from your current situation but God is the God of the past, present, and future. He has a good plan for those who love Him. "And we know that all things work together for good to those who love God, to those who are the called according to His purpose" (Rom. 8:28).

FINAL THOUGHT

We have all certainly heard the famous hymn "Just As I Am" by Charlotte Elliott (1789-1871). Billy Graham used this hymn to conclude his Evangelist Crusades. He would give a simple invitation: "If the Lord is speaking to your heart, come to the front and receive Him as your savior. Your new life can begin tonight." Hundreds would respond.

I want to extend the same invitation to you. Listen to the words and respond in faith to the message of salvation.

Just as I am, without one plea,
but that thy blood was shed for me,
and that thou bidd'st me come to thee,
O Lamb of God, I come, I come.

Just as I am, and waiting not
to rid my soul of one dark blot,
to thee, whose blood can cleanse each spot,
O Lamb of God, I come, I come.

Just as I am, though tossed about
with many a conflict, many a doubt,
fightings and fears within, without,
O Lamb of God, I come, I come.

Just as I am, thou wilt receive,
wilt welcome, pardon, cleanse, relieve;
because thy promise I believe,
O Lamb of God, I come, I come.

Our lives are passing like a parade. Daily thousands die in the United States; many are young, many more are older. Death is the transition from earth into eternity. Our destination is determined by our relationship with Christ.

The following series of verses are called the Romans Road through scripture to understand salvation. Notes were written by Brian Tubbs (https://pastorbriantubbs.com).

1—"As it is written: 'There is none righteous, no, not one.'" (Rom. 3:10)

Quoting from the Psalms, the apostle Paul declares here that no single human being is "righteous" (the meaning of which is best understood as "right with God").

2—"For all have sinned, and fall short of the glory of God." (Rom. 3:23)

Lest someone protest that they are a good person, especially when compared to people they know or observe in the news or in their workplace (or wherever), Paul points out that the standard isn't your neighbor, but rather God Himself. It isn't enough that you compare yourself to another human being and think, "Well, I'm not as bad as he is." The standard is God's holiness. And all of us fall short of that standard.

3—"For the wages of sin is death, but the gift of God is eternal life in Christ Jesus our Lord." (Rom. 6:23)

Having established that we are all sinners who fall short of God's glory, Paul explains that the "wages" (or earnings) of our sin is "death." This includes both physical death and spiritual death. Physical death is when your soul separates from your body.

Spiritual death is when your soul is separated from God. And this separation from God extends into eternity for those who die in their lost and sinful state.

Because of our sin, we face the reality and inevitability of both physical death and eternal separation from God. Paul, however, doesn't leave us with just bad news. He mentions that the "gift of God" is "eternal life through Jesus Christ our Lord."

And to further explain this, we step back a chapter in Romans to go to the next milestone marker in the Romans Road.

4—"But God demonstrates His own love toward us, in that while we were still sinners, Christ died for us." (Rom. 5:8)

God doesn't leave us in our sinful state. He doesn't leave us with the prospect of facing both physical and spiritual death. There is, as they say, "more to the story."

Paul says that God demonstrated or commended (gave) love to us even when we didn't deserve it. Even when we were deep in sin, "Christ died for us."

What do we do with this information? Well, for that, we come to the final passage of the Romans Road.

5—For "whoever calls on the name of the Lord shall be saved." (Rom. 10:13)

The bad news is we all fall short of God's glory and we all face both physical and spiritual death because of it. The good news is that God loved us, sent Jesus to die for us, and anyone who calls upon "the name of the Lord shall be saved."

For a deeper explanation of what it means to call on the name of the Lord, Romans 10:13 should be read and understood in the context of the verses which precede it.

If you want to understand what it takes to have your sins forgiven, to be saved by God, and thus have your place with God in eternity firmly established, Romans 10:9-13 is perhaps the clearest explanation in all the Bible — with the exception of Jesus' conversation with Nicodemus in the third chapter of the Gospel of John.

We must communicate to God our clear declaration that Jesus is Lord and we must believe that Jesus rose from the dead. This must be a sincere, intentional head-and-heart decision we make before God. And those who are genuine and authentic in their confession of Christ and profession of faith "shall not be ashamed."

This passage also makes clear that all of humanity (both "the Jew and the Greek" — referring to Jew and Gentile, which in biblical terms, comprises the whole of humanity) is loved by God and is eligible for this offer of salvation. God will hear anyone who calls on the name of His Son as Lord.

And there you have it! That is the Romans Road to Salvation.

REVIEW

I am a visual learner. Present me with a long list of facts or figures and I can quickly become overwhelmed with what I need to know or remember. However, present the same data in a graph or other visual form and I can not only mentally "see" relationships and trends but also remember them quite well. Dr. Ferry's *Finding Fellowship – A Visualized Study of Philemon* does just that for me in the study of God's Word.

Finding Fellowship – A Visualized Study of Philemon is a short treatise on the Apostle Paul's spiritual relationship to Philemon, and based on that relationship, Paul's wish for Philemon's relationship to Onesimus, his former slave. Interwoven throughout the short twenty-five verses of the Book of Philemon are the threads of many doctrinal subjects such as Christian fellowship, acceptance, forgiveness, and family. Dr. Ferry masterfully exposes and follows these threads in Paul's letter to Philemon.

Whether Dr. Ferry intended it or not, I found *Finding Fellowship* to be a first-rate beginning tutorial on biblical applications. I enjoyed following Dr. Ferry's method of extracting simple, but thoughtful, applications from each verse and then applying them to a modern Christian audience through a visual media.

I recommend *Finding Fellowship – A Visualized Study of Philemon* to everyone interested in a concise, visual, biblical analysis of the Book of Philemon.

Mr. Ronn Dunn
Bible Class Instructor
Triad Baptist Church

69

REVIEW

First, I would like to say that Dr. Ferry makes excellent use of definitions throughout his book, *Finding Fellowship – A Visualized Study of Philemon*. For example, early on, he defines the word "grace" as "*unmerited favor: kindness without expected return*" and the word "peace" as "*condition of enjoyable existence without conflict.*" This approach helped me to better understand his teaching that in order to have peace in the church it is necessary to first have grace in the church. Having been an active church member for most of my life, I recognize this as a simple yet profound truth. Without contemplation of the definitions offered in this book I fear that I might overlook the depth of insights presented by the author.

Secondly, pointing out key words found in the passages helps the reader to ponder more deeply what the apostle Paul was striving to communicate to Philemon, the recipient of the letter. This is a great help for those readers and learners who are not so inclined to distinguish such particulars on their own.

Thirdly, provocative questions are included both throughout the book and in abundance in the last section where several sets of admirable discussion questions are offered for small groups or study classes. A wonderful use of these could be directed to learners who are incarcerated just as the apostle Paul was when he wrote the Letter to Philemon. These questions will no doubt help the reader learn more effectively.

Fourthly, this book would be an excellent resource for Pastors and Bible teachers looking to teach the truths of Philemon to their respective flocks. Individuals would also enjoy the information found in the book just as I did. My understanding has increased both for personal devotion to the Lord Jesus Christ and for sharing with others to help them grow in grace.

In closing, Dr. Ferry has made rich use of other Biblical Scripture passages outside of Philemon in support of the apostle Paul's statements as well as his own notions and assertions to help the reader mature in knowledge and understanding of the personal correspondence of Paul to Philemon on behalf of a new and dear Christian named Onesimus. I applaud the author and hope that others will enjoy and benefit from this brief study as I have.

Mr. Donald Culbertson
Bible Class Instructor
Triad Baptist Church

REVIEW

Dr. Ferry's *Finding Fellowship – A Visualized Study of Philemon* is a unique look at the book of Philemon. He goes through Philemon exegetically and gives practical application throughout. It is filled with helpful visuals that clarify applications.

Fellowship, I believe, can be improved and made more effective in all our churches. People often mistake acquaintances for fellowship, so they miss the biblical meaning of it. Dr. Ferry guides us through the book and we see what the Apostle Paul wanted to teach us about "Finding Fellowship."

Mr. Paul Jayne
High School Bible Teacher
Triad Baptist Christian Academy

BOOKS BY THE AUTHOR

A MAN & HIS COUNTRY, 2007

What does the Bible teach by example and principle about a man and authority? How do military service, war, and civil servanthood reconcile with God's Word? What does the Bible teach about politics? What does the Bible teach about civil disobedience? What about a man's responsibility as a citizen of Heaven? This 8-chapter study will help you discover what the Bible teaches about these issues and more. A Man and His Country will challenge you to be the kind of citizen God wants you to be.

WISDOM FOR WARRIORS, 2017

Sixty devotionals from Proverbs delivered to the Aviation Brigade while the author deployed during Operation Iraqi Freedom III.

THREADS OF FAMILY, FAITH & FLAG, 2017

Allen Ferry and co-author Greg Masiello are combat veterans who served together during Operation Iraqi Freedom (2004-05). This book was conceived when they recognized that their shared patriotism was birthed from generational love for family, faith and the flag. They write from personal experiences that shaped their lives for military service. Journeys have been different but both are thrilled that their fellowship is based on a personal relationship with the Lord.

They hope your patriotism will be increased as you travel with them from their home towns, get to know their families, live through Iraq, and into retirement.

INSIGHTS FROM INSIDE: CHAPLAINCY & CORRECTIONS, 2018

This insightful and personal treatment of prison ministry and Chaplaincy maintains a spiritual edge and is grounded in reality and honesty. It is a compilation of resources and vignettes from many sources that adds to its effectiveness. Bottom line of all the contributors is that Chaplains in correctional settings need to "keep it real" when there, and be themselves and "not someone else" including wearing a religious or intellectual mask. Prisoners and those working in prisons can see though masks quickly and the credibility of the Chaplain is compromised easily. If you are looking for a straightforward current treatment of the subject, there is enough material here to meet that need. — Dr. Michael Nace

REFLECTIONS OF GRACE: CHRISTLIKE MEN AND WOMEN WHO INFLUENCED MY LIFE, 2019

"Reflections of Grace" is a compelling testimony to God's grace and faithfulness in the life of my friend Allen Douglas Ferry. God promised Israel in Isaiah 61:3 to give beauty for ashes for His glory. He still does that today. As Doug walked through the ashes of his parents' divorce, his health challenges, and the disappointment of the possibly closed door to chaplaincy, God brought into his life godly men and women who were instrumental in turning those ashes into beauty. Reflections of Grace is a chronology of the ministry of those men and women in Doug's life that enabled him to touch the lives of so many others.

My wife and I have known Doug and Theresa for over 50 years. It was my joy to walk beside him in his Chaplaincy ministry and to observe God's hand on their lives. From the ashes of Ground Zero and deployments to combat zones, to the ashes of broken lives in correctional institutions, I have observed God using Doug as he helped others turn the ashes of their lives into beauty for God's glory.

I count it a privilege to have Doug as a friend, colleague, and fellow servant. May the lives referenced in this book challenge us to live for God's glory so that others will see in us Reflections of Grace. — Dr. John B. Murdoch

THAT REMINDS ME OF A STORY, 2020

A good illustration by story telling is like putting a window into a building that otherwise is without much light. This taught me to almost always use stories to help people under- stand the point of the message. Illustrations were from other biblical texts, sometimes by current events, and daily life.

My expression, "That reminds me of a story" has become the target of much humor. Some have decided they should number my stories and save the time needed to tell them! In any case, my friends know the point of my stories; each puts a "window" into the house of the discussion.

This book is a compilation of personal stories. Some have never been told before; some have been told many times over many years. I hope that these will put a smile on your face, a thought in your heart, or a principle in your mind for future use.

LIFE IS A PASSING PARADE, 2021

Karen Wagner Swanson and Allen Douglas Ferry (co-authors) are 1965 graduates of Warren Area High School, Warren, Pennsylvania. As years pass, they realize the significance of viewing everything through the lens of eternity.

By combining individual writing skills, their intent is to emphasize the importance of a personal relationship with Christ and life lived for Him. They realize that our lives are much like a passing parade.

Karen taught Bible Study Fellowship classes for 25 years and continues to lead educational tours of Israel. She recently authored Mom Mail. She lives with her husband, Lanny, in Fort Collins, CO. They have three adult children and several grandchildren.

Allen served as a pastor, as an Army (Colonel) Chaplain and also a Bible College director. He has authored several books, most recently, *Reflections of Grace* and *That Reminds Me of a Story*. He lives with his wife, Theresa, in Kernersville, NC. They have two adult children and three grandchildren.

A BREATH OF FRESH AIR, 2022

A tribute to special men and women who have been B.O.F.A.(s) in the author's life. Not all are noted; some have passed through my life quickly. Some have been lost in my memories.

All titles are available on Amazon

Made in the USA
Monee, IL
05 November 2024